WINTER DAYS FOR CARDINALS

A Novel for Children

by

Katharine (Kit) Kohudic

DORRANCE
PUBLISHING CO
EST. 1920
PITTSBURGH, PENNSYLVANIA 15238

Dorrance Publishing Co
585 Alpha Drive, Suite 103
Pittsburgh, PA 15238
Visit our website at *www.dorrancebooks.com*

ISBN: 978-1-4809-5500-4
eISBN: 978-1-4809-5477-9

Chapter 1 – Winter Morning

Although the sun was shining, it wasn't adding much warmth to the neighborhood. A pair of cardinals were snuggled together, deep within the big, blue spruce tree that sat in the corner of the Krell's backyard. The male cardinal, Henry, awakened first and made his way toward the end of the sturdy branches to see what might be happening. The snow that had fallen during the night was glittering in the sunlight, making everything appear clean and fresh. All was very quiet until he heard little chirps and the beginning of a song coming from the nearby bushes and trees.

Henry was covered with a coat of brilliant red feathers with a red crest on the very top of his head that stood straight up as he strained to listen to the sounds. Even his thick beak was red, but the area around his face and down his front was black, making for a handsome color combination.

His mate, Meg, was soon perched on a nearby branch and together, they scanned the backyard for any signs of movement. Meg was the same size as Henry, but her feathers were a dull, gray-orange in color with just a bit of red in her wings, tail, and crest. She, too, heard the rustling sounds of the neighborhood's wildlife awakening to a new day. A squirrel scampered down one of the trees in front of the big, white house, dashed across the street, and disappeared from view.

In the middle of the yard stood a black pole with a wooden birdfeeder on top. The feeder was empty, but the young boy who lived in the house had appeared almost every morning to fill it with a mixture of seeds. It was the sunflower seeds that Henry and Meg liked the best. Their heavy, strong bills were able to crack open the shells with ease, and the seeds were definitely worth the effort.

"I'm thinking of flying over to the park, Meg. Do you want to come with me?" Henry asked.

"Go on, Henry," said Meg. "I'll wait a bit to see if the boy brings out the can with crumbs and seeds."

Henry flew low over the singing wires and the snow covered rooftops, keeping a look out for other wildlife in the neighborhood. A few dogs had been let out to play in the snow, but he didn't see a single cat. Some chickadees and other small birds were flitting among the lower bushes and a pair of mourning doves was perched near the chimney of a house for warmth.

He flew over the elementary school, scanning the deserted schoolyard, and through the evergreen trees that marked the entrance to the park. The park wasn't large, but it was usually a good place to often find berries and seeds during the winter months.

Henry had just found a clutch of red berries when he heard the rat-tat-tat-tat sound of a woodpecker echoing through the park. He gobbled a few of the berries and flew toward the noise. As he perched on a branch of a tree, he spotted Pete, a Red-bellied Woodpecker, whose tummy was indeed a light reddish color. The back and top of his head were also red, while his back and wing feathers were covered with black and white stripes. Pete was very busy drilling into a dead tree trunk in search of hidden insects.

"Hey, Pete," squawked Henry, "are you finding anything?"

"Oh, hi, Henry," said Pete, "Yup, yup, I've got a tasty spider in here somewhere." Rat-tat-tat-tat. "Found some good, sticky sap, too." Rat-tat-tat-tat. "Yup, good stuff here, friend, good stuff here." Rat-tat-tat-tat.

Henry let the woodpecker continue his search of the dead tree and flew to a nearby pond. The pond was frozen, but apparently, some raccoons or skunks had recently dug a small hole in the ice, and there was just enough water for Henry to get a drink.

Henry flew back to the Krell's backyard, but heard a distinctive CHEE CHEE CHEE CHEE before he even made it to the big, blue spruce tree. That was Fletcher's call, all right, and Henry knew the big blue jay must have his feathers ruffled about something. Then he spotted the trouble.

Meg and two chickadees were perched on one side of the now full birdfeeder, but on the other side of the feeder, another cardinal and his mate were grabbing sunflower seeds and cracking them open as fast as possible.

When Fletcher spotted Henry, he called out to say, "It's not right, Henry! There won't be enough seeds for you and Meg and the others if that new pair of cardinals stays here much longer. It's just not fair, I tell you!"

Henry didn't respond to Fletcher, but flew directly at the male cardinal, trying to bump him off the feeder. Meg and the other birds flew to safety as the two male cardinals flew at each other in anger. When the stranger and his mate flew to a nearby tree branch, Henry flew back to the top of the feeder and announced that this was his feeder and the newcomers could just find some other place for breakfast.

"What's your name, anyway?" asked Henry when he had settled down a bit.

"I'm Nelson," said the red male cardinal, "and this is my mate, Singer. We'll find a better feeder somewhere else for now, but be warned—we'll be back. You won't run us off so easily next time."

As the pair flew away, Meg joined Henry at the feeder. For some reason, the feeder felt rather wobbly and unsteady as they began to crack open the sunflower seeds, side by side.

With all the excitement, many of the smaller seeds had been knocked to the ground. The black-capped chickadees and juncos hopped around the depressions left in the snow under the feeder by the boy's big boots, finding plenty to eat.

"Whew," said Fletcher, "that was not a good start on our day. I think I'll follow that gray squirrel, and maybe he'll lead me to his stash of acorns. That would fill my bill!"

The sun was shining brightly in the clear, blue sky, and there was hope that the snow would melt just enough to provide water for the feathered folk in the neighborhood.

CHAPTER 2 – FRIENDS AND STRANGERS

BANG! The back door of the Krell's house slammed shut as Jimmy took off his snowy boots, left them on the mat to dry, and entered the kitchen. Unaware that the birds were fighting at the feeder, Jimmy sat down in front of a stack of pancakes his mother had put at his place at the breakfast table. His father was preparing to leave for work and his younger sister, Sherry, was using her fork to make designs in the leftover syrup on her plate.

"Mommy," said Sherry, "don't forget that today is Friday, and I'm going over to Bonnie's house tonight for a sleepover."

"Come home first after school today, and we'll make sure you have everything you need to take with you," replied her mother.

"Bonnie just lives around the corner," said Jimmy, "it isn't like she's taking a trip!"

Mr. Krell got up from the table and said, "I seem to remember when you first started having sleepovers at Donald's house; you wanted to take all your toys and sports gear with you, and Donald just lives up the street."

"Oh, Dad, Donald and I are ten now, so it's not like when we were babies!" said Jimmy, looking right at Sherry.

"I'm NOT a baby," cried Sherry. "Bonnie and I are best friends, and we're going to play together all day tomorrow."

"Good," Jimmy said. "It's nice to know you won't be following me and Donald around all day."

Mrs. Krell stepped into the middle of the conversation and announced that the children's lunches were packed, and they would need to start their walk to school soon.

As Mr. Krell was getting into the car to go to work, Jimmy and Sherry were racing up the stairs, giggling and laughing as they went. It was a typical day at the Krell's house.

By noon, the sun was strong enough to melt some of the snow, and the feathered folk found plenty of places to get a drink of water. Even the Krell's cat, Jake, was outside. The front porch was covered, so it made for a nice, dry place to sit and sniff the air. He could hear chirping sounds and when a bird flew right in front of him, Jake would crouch down and growl. He wasn't about to venture down the steps, which were wet from the snow melting, and he certainly didn't like the snow.

Jake couldn't see the backyard from the front porch, so he didn't see the birds flitting from bush to tree to the top of the swing set. The little chickadees and juncos were enjoying the sunshine and cleaning their wings while Fletcher and the bigger birds seemed to be sharing bits of news.

"Hey," squawked Fletcher as he landed on a branch of the blue spruce tree near Henry and Meg. "Guess who I saw?"

Henry cocked his head to the side and said, "Um, that orange cat isn't around, is he?"

"Nope," replied Fletcher. "I saw him out on the front porch, but I don't think he likes the snow, so we should be all right."

"Okay," said Meg. "Who did you see?"

"Well, I know the daylight seems to be lasting longer and Kate, Ringo, and the others who migrate south for the winter won't be back for awhile, but I think I saw Mert."

"Mert?" questioned Henry. "It's too early for that old yellow warbler to be here."

"That's what I thought," replied Fletcher, "it's too early for any of the summer crowd. The snow is melting a little, but I bet we'll get more before the season is over."

"You know," said Meg, "I wasn't sure we'd even be seeing Mert again. He's getting older, and I know he flies a great distance twice a year."

"Well," said Fletcher, "I'm just telling you what I thought I saw. Maybe I'll take a tour of the neighborhood and see what I can see."

After Fletcher flew off, Henry and Meg spent some time cleaning their feathers and then went in search for water. As they flew by the front of the house, they could see someone holding the front door open and an orange, striped tail disappeared inside. Jake knew the sun would be shining on the back of the living room sofa, just the right place for a well-deserved nap!

"Look," cried Meg, "there he is, there's Mert, toward the top of the cherry tree. I'd recognize those yellow feathers and thin, pointy bill anywhere."

Meg and Henry flew over the top of the light brown colored house and settled on a bare branch of the cherry tree that grew in the backyard.

"Hi, Henry and hi, Meg," Mert chirped.

"Well, hello, Mert," said Henry. "We're just a little surprised to see you back so early. Did you get tired of all that warm weather?"

Mert warbled a bit to clear his throat and said, "Not really. It's just that I'm not as young and strong as I used to be, and I decided to get an early start on the trip north. I haven't found much to eat, and I'm going to need some berries or something to keep me warm tonight."

"I know just the place," said Henry. "You remember Pete the woodpecker, I'm sure. He's been finding some tasty things in the park beyond the schoolyard, follow me."

As the friends flew off, Meg returned to the blue spruce tree in time to see the children return home from school. She was glad that the children didn't seem to be much of a threat to the wildlife in the neighborhood. She did notice, however, that the wind was starting to blow, and it definitely felt colder.

Inside the house, the Krell children had shed their winter jackets and left their schoolbooks on the stairs. Jimmy was on the telephone with his friend Donald while Sherry and her mother were in the kitchen, choosing some snacks that Sherry wanted to share with Bonnie. Then mother and daughter went up the stairs to pack Sherry a small, overnight bag.

"I have to take my pillow, Mom," said Sherry. "I can't fall asleep without it—and my teddy bear, of course."

Mrs. Krell and Sherry managed to get everything Sherry needed for the sleepover into the car in only two trips, and soon they were on their way around the block.

Meanwhile, Jimmy and Donald had decided to spend the rest of the afternoon trying to build a snowman in the Krell's backyard before all the snow melted.

Neither the Krell's nor the feathered folk had any idea that some big changes were on their way. Changes that would affect birds and people alike.

CHAPTER 3 – SURPRISE ATTACK

By the time Mr. Krell arrived home from work, his wife had returned home from taking Sherry to her friend's house, and the boys were busy trying to build a snowman. Actually, the wet snow made for good packing, and a rather lopsided snowman was taking shape.

Two older boys, Sam and Ralph, were also outside. They lived across the street from the blue house and were never too friendly with the younger children. Before leaving for school in the morning, the boys had made several snowballs and put them in the freezer, which sat in the basement of Ralph's house. Those iceballs were going to be the boys' special ammunition.

Jimmy and Donald had thrown a few snow-balls themselves as they worked on rolling up the snow for the base of their snowman. Their gloves were wet, and somehow snow had landed inside Jimmy's left boot, making his sock cold and wet.

What they didn't know was that Sam and Ralph were on the other side of the wall that separated the Krell's backyard from the sidewalk. They were busily making rows of snowballs and had their special iceballs on the side.

"There," said Donald, "we've got the middle of our snowman pretty well cemented in place. Now all we need is one more ball of snow for the head."

"I can get a carrot for the nose and maybe borrow a hat from my dad," said Jimmy, "but I'm not sure what we'll use to make a mouth."

"Let's get this snow rolling first," replied Donald, "and then . . . hey, I thought we agreed to stop throwing snowballs until we had the snowman done!"

"I didn't throw any snowball," said Jimmy. "Yikes—I got hit, too! What's going on around here?"

More snowballs flew over the wall, and Jimmy could hear laughter coming from the other side. Donald ran over to the wall and spied Sam and Ralph. They were picking up one snowball after another from their stash, and Donald managed to duck just in time to keep from being hit in the face.

Jimmy and Donald sprang into action, grabbing handfuls of snow, packing it into balls as quickly as possible, and lobbing them over the wall. Hits were made on both sides and when Ralph's hat was knocked off, he grabbed an iceball, stepped back to aim at Donald, and threw it as hard as he could. Donald ducked at the last moment and . . . CRASH!

The iceball hit the bird feeder, tearing it off the pole, and sending pieces flying in all directions. The small seeds that had been on the bottom of the feeder landed in a pile on the ground.

Jimmy was really angry now and stood next to the wall, raining down snowballs at Sam and Ralph as fast as he could make and throw. No longer having fun, Sam and Ralph switched to using all their homemade iceballs. The last iceball they threw hit Jimmy in the forehead, and he fell to the ground. Sam and Ralph looked at each other with big eyes and started to run back home.

"Jimmy," shouted Donald as he started to shake his friend, "Jimmy, are you all right? Can you get up? Come on, Jimmy, say something!"

Jimmy's eyes fluttered open, and there were tears forming as he looked at Donald and touched his head with a snowy mitten. "I think I'm okay, but my head really hurts."

Jimmy sat up and suddenly realized how wet and cold he had become. He twisted his head to look at what was left of the bird feeder and started to get up.

"Hold on to me," said Donald. "We'll worry about the feeder later, but right now we had better get inside the house."

"Okay," said Jimmy, "let's go."

Once inside the backdoor, the boys struggled with cold hands to remove their gloves, boots, jackets, and hats. The boys knew the rule of the house—when anyone came inside with snowy boots and jackets, they were to take them down into the basement and hang any wet clothing on the clothesline. This time, however, the boys threw their outerwear and boots down the steps and went looking for Jimmy's parents.

Mrs. Krell saw Jimmy first and made him sit down on a kitchen chair so she could get a better look at his head. She sent Donald off to locate Mr. Krell as she examined the large, growing bump on Jimmy's forehead. It was very red, but she didn't see any blood. Mr. Krell came through the kitchen door with a look of concern on his face, followed by Donald.

"Is he all right?" asked Mr. Krell.

"He seems to be okay," said Mrs. Krell. "His eyes are clear, but he's got quite a goose egg on his forehead."

"And a headache!" said Jimmy, quietly.

Donald couldn't keep quiet. "It was an ice ball, I tell you. Sam and Ralph just didn't play fair. They wrecked the bird feeder and everything."

"Okay," said Mr. Krell. "Have some hot chocolate while I call Dr. Winn. Then, I want to hear the whole story."

After putting a plate of cookies in front of the boys, Mrs. Krell went to work fixing the hot chocolate. It didn't take long for the boys to feel warmer and start to relax.

Mr. Krell returned and said, "The nurse in Dr. Winn's office said that as long as there wasn't any bleeding and Jimmy's eyes were clear, he would probably be all right. We can give him some aspirin, but we should keep an eye on him for now."

Mrs. Krell had made an ice bag and asked Jimmy to hold it on his head. Then Jimmy spoke up for the first time, "The bird feeder! Those bullies destroyed our bird feeder!"

"Okay," said Mr. Krell as he sat at the kitchen table with the boys, "Let's hear the whole story. I need to know exactly what happened out there."

Jimmy and Donald told about making the snowman, the sneak snowball attack by the older boys, and how the fun had changed to a real fight when Sam and Ralph had started to hurl ice balls.

"Donald," said Mr. Krell, "come out back with me, and let's see if we can locate one of those ice balls, just to prove it."

Donald ran down the basement steps to retrieve his boots and jacket and led the way to the scene of the crime. Meanwhile, Jimmy took two aspirin and curled up on the sofa in the living room, still holding the ice bag to his forehead. He heard his father and best friend come into the house and go right to the kitchen. He could tell they opened the freezer section of the refrigerator because the freezer door made a very distinct swoosh noise whenever Jimmy was looking for ice cream.

Donald found Jimmy on the couch and said that they had indeed found most of what was left of one of the ice balls and it was now sitting in the Krell's freezer. However, he didn't tell Jimmy that the bird feeder was in too many little pieces to ever be put back together again. He knew Jimmy was an avid bird watcher and cared about their welfare.

The sun had set and the air was definitely colder, so Mr. Krell walked with Donald back to his house to make sure he got home safely. Then, after dinner, the Krell's spent the evening on the sofa together with Jake sitting comfortably on Mrs. Krell's lap. They watched a movie on TV and for once, Jimmy was glad to go to bed.

An hour later, Jake was the first to hear it—an unusual sound on the roof and small, pinging sounds on the windows. He trotted to the front door because it had a long, clear pane of glass on one side, but it was too dark outside to see anything. Mrs. Krell heard it, too. She put down the dishtowel she was using to dry the dishes and met Jake at the front door. She turned around and pushed the switch that turned on the porch light.

Neither Mrs. Krell nor Jake moved. They stood together watching the small pellets of ice hit the porch, steps, and walkway. It was raining ice! Jake backed away as if the icy rain might try to come inside the house. Mrs. Krell hunted for her husband and together, they put candles and matches in strategic locations around the house in case they lost power from the storm. Then they went to bed and tried to get to sleep. Jimmy was probably the only one to sleep well that night, unaware of the storm or the fact that Jake had taken refuge at the foot of his bed.

Chapter 4 - Saturday

The icy branches of the blue spruce tree rattled as Henry and Meg emerged the next morning from their dry, protected spot near the trunk. The sky was cloudy and the air very cold. What they saw as they peered between the icicles was awesome.

It seemed like the whole world had changed overnight. Even without the sunshine, the layer of ice that covered everything was glistening. What used to be fluffy white snow now wore a thick, icy crust. The swing set was coated in ice and icicles hung from the roof of the Krell's house. Every twig on every bush and tree had its own, individual coat of ice, making the backyard look like a fairyland.

"Henry," said Meg, "what happened to the feeder? All I see is the black pole."

"I don't know, Meg," replied Henry.

"There was all that noise from the children, but it was hard to tell exactly what was going on."

"I know!" chirped Fletcher as he tried to get a footing on a nearby ice clad branch. "It was those boys. They were throwing lots of snow around and from the roof of the house, I heard a big noise—like something breaking and falling apart. When the kids finally left the yard, I swooped down for a look. I'm sorry to tell you that there were pieces of the feeder lying on the ground."

"Oh no," said Henry. "Just when we'll need the feeder the most, it's gone."

"But did you notice that just under the ice at the foot of the pole there's a pile of seeds?" asked Fletcher. "I tried to chip away at the ice with my bill, but that ice is just too tough."

"What about Pete?" asked Meg, "maybe he could break it up, and at least the smaller birds could have it."

"Good idea, Meg," said Fletcher. "I think I'll see if I can find him. I'll catch up with you two later today."

Henry thought for a moment and said, "I'll do a bit of searching for another feeder that might be open, Meg, and come back to get you—okay?"

"Just take care with all this ice, dear," said Meg as she fluffed out her feathers in an effort to stay warm.

Fletcher did find Pete, who was trying to fasten his talons on the icy trunk of a tree by the schoolyard.

"Fletch, have you ever seen anything like this ice?" squawked Pete. "I think I've found a spot on this tree that is pretty clear, but it's hard to find any bugs this time of year."

Fletcher explained to Pete the problem of the ice covered seed pile at the Krell's house, and Pete agreed to give it a try. They didn't see much activity as they flew over the icy neighborhood. It was like everything had come to a stand still.

Meg watched from her perch as the two birds skidded on the ice upon landing and began hopping and clawing their way to the buried seed pile. Pete went to work, stabbing his sharp bill repeatedly into the ice. He was able to break the ice into small chunks, which sent Fletcher flying out of the way.

It wasn't long before the quiet of the morning was broken by a continuous call of CHEE CHEE CHEE CHEE CHEE CHEE! The feathered folk all knew there was either trouble brewing or something of importance going on.

Pete stepped back to admire his work and soon the sparrows, chickadees, and even a shy tufted titmouse were grabbing at the seeds as fast as they could. Fletcher was quite proud of having a part in such a grand accomplishment. He hadn't found anything to eat yet, and those little seeds certainly wouldn't satisfy a big fellow like himself, so he was thinking it was time to try a raid on the squirrel's nest he knew of in the next block.

Having done his good deed, Pete also flew off to find bigger nuts or seeds.

After Henry left the blue spruce tree, his first stop was at the cherry tree. As he clung to a swaying, ice-covered branch, he looked into the yard of the blue house next door. He knew it was too cold and icy for the dog, Chance, to be outside, but he was hoping someone had thrown some breadcrumbs on the ground. No crumbs, so Henry flew over all the houses in the block and knew he would fly even farther. If the ice and cold lasted more than another day, the lives of all the feathered folk would be endangered.

When Jimmy awakened that same Saturday morning, he touched his forehead to make sure that everything that had happened wasn't just a bad dream. The lump he found was indeed real. He lay in bed and wondered what had happened to the snowman and thought he should start planning some kind of revenge on Sam and Ralph. It wasn't until he looked out his bedroom window that he saw the results of the overnight ice storm.

Jake was awakened as the boy got up out of bed. After washing a paw, he leaped down to the floor and made his way down the stairs, looking for breakfast.

Jimmy's parents were already at the kitchen table. Mr. Krell, having watched the latest weather report, announced that the whole city was shut down, and they were asking people to not attempt driving until the roads were cleared. There seemed to be a glimmer of hope that the sun would be shining in the afternoon, and perhaps the ice would begin to melt.

Just then the telephone rang. Mrs. Krell was pretty sure that it was Sherry calling from Bonnie's house.

"Mom," said Sherry, "have you seen all the ice? Isn't it beautiful? We're having eggs and toast this morning, and Bonnie's father says we can't go outside yet, but we're going to have a tea party with our dolls inside anyway. Do I have to come home now?"

"Not with all this ice, dear," laughed Mrs. Krell. "If Bonnie's family can put up with you a little longer, we'll make it up to them later. Just behave yourself, and we'll come to get you when we can."

Mother and daughter talked a bit more and when Mrs. Krell hung up the telephone, she almost stumbled over the big, orange, striped cat who was wrapping his tail around her legs.

Jimmy's head still hurt, but he certainly felt better after breakfast. He thought for a moment, and said, "Dad, can I get on the Internet and look for bird feeders? I don't know how the birds are going to find anything to eat with all this ice."

"Okay, son, see what you can find and let me know. I doubt the hardware store will be open today, though."

"And, Mom," continued Jimmy, "can we find some bread or cracker crumbs and at least throw them out the back door?"

"I'm sure I can find something for your feathered friends," Mrs. Krell replied.

The sun remained hidden all day long, so the temperature never rose above freezing. The city trucks worked diligently to keep the main highways open, leaving the residential streets untouched. It made the neighborhood a quiet place, with the wildlife settled down and doing the only thing they could do—wait.

Chapter 5 - Sunday

Sunday morning dawned with clear, bright sunshine, but with temperatures still below freezing, the layer of ice continued to dominate the scene. Trucks had worked through the night to dump salt and sand on the streets and scrape away the slush, making them at least passable for those who could get their cars out of their own driveways.

Thus, some churches were open to the faithful who attempted the drive.

Jimmy was feeling better, but his parents would not allow him to go outside yet. He called Donald, and they had a big discussion about the snowball fight, the broken bird feeder, and their headless snowman. They agreed that they needed to do something to get back at the bullies, but couldn't come up with a solid plan—yet.

Mr. Krell had been surprised to hear the sound of the Sunday newspaper landing on the front porch late in the morning. As he stepped outside to retrieve it, he could see that the street had been cleared and the rock salt he had spread on the steps and sidewalk had started to work on the ice.

Mrs. Krell and Bonnie's mother had agreed that Sherry could probably make it home on foot, if she was careful. Jimmy was volunteered by his mother to walk over and help Sherry carry at least some of her things home.

First, of course, Mrs. Krell would have to get Jimmy off the computer.

"But, Mom," Jimmy complained, "I'm doing important research on bird feeders. I think I've found just the one, and I want to talk it over with Dad."

"Your father is deep into the Sunday paper just now, but maybe when you get back you both can look at the feeders," Mrs. Krell suggested. "Besides, we really don't know the condition of the sidewalks around the corner, and your little sister needs you."

'Little sisters are a pain the neck,' thought Jimmy as he made his way around the corner. Most people had at least made an attempt to clear their sidewalks, but there were still icy patches that he had to step around.

"Okay, Jimmy," said Sherry, as she handed him her overnight bag while she carried her pillow and her teddy bear. "Let's roll!"

What normally took five minutes now took much longer as the children walked carefully along. Sherry carried her pillow and bear in one hand, leaving her other hand to grab on to Jimmy if she should slip on the ice.

They turned the corner and were walking past the brown house when something caught Jimmy's eye. It was a small patch of bright yellow lying on the ice-covered grass between the sidewalk and the street.

"What are you looking at, Jimmy?" asked Sherry as they stopped.

"I'm not sure, Sis, but it looks like— well, maybe a bird," said Jimmy. "Gee, it is a bird, and it must be dead because it isn't moving."

"Oh, no," said Sherry, "the poor thing must have frozen to death. What can we do?"

Jimmy replied, "I'm not sure we can do anything. It seems to be stuck in the ice. We'll just have to let Mother Nature take care of it."

"And what is Mother Nature going to do?" asked Sherry.

"Well, I don't know everything," admitted Jimmy, "but I bet if we look for the bird again in a few days after it warms up it will be gone."

"My nose is cold," said Sherry, "let's just go on home."

The children walked the rest of the way in silence, each considering the poor, yellow bird entrapped in the ice.

Chapter 6 – Winter Hangs On

As usual, it was the feathered folk who first noticed just a bit of change in the air. The sun shone high in the bright, blue sky as Henry and Meg were perched on the end of one of the branches of their spruce tree.

"Did you knock a piece of ice on me?" chirped Meg as she shook her feathers.

"Not me," said Henry, "I thought I felt a drop of water, too. And look, Fletcher is standing tall on top of the swing set—that means the ice must be starting to melt!"

The cardinal couple flew over to join their friend on the swing set.

"Hey, you two," said Fletcher, rather hesitantly, "Um . . . you know . . . I've got some news to report."

Meg could see Fletcher was not his usual noisy self. "What's with you today, are you all right?"

"I'm all right," said Fletcher, "but you two need to know . . . well, just follow me, and I'll show you."

Henry and Meg followed Fletcher as he flew around the blue spruce tree, over the fence, and alighted on the other side of the sidewalk that ran in front of the brown house. It was still a bit icy, so the three slid to a stop near a yellow mound sticking up out of the ice.

Meg was the first to speak, "Oh dear, it's Mert, isn't it?"

"I'm afraid so," said Fletcher.

Henry was quiet for a moment, then said, "I'm sorry for you, Mert, old friend. You made it back to the neighborhood all right, but it was just too early."

"We'll miss you and your lovely music," added Meg.

Fletcher said, "I thought you two ought to know about this. Mert was quite old, but if we get any more ice, others will die as well."

"That's true, Fletch," said Henry, "it's melting enough to get water. I spotted a feeder behind a house over near the schoolyard that looked promising. We had better check it out, Meg."

The cardinals went on their way, and Fletcher joined some of the other birds that were enjoying a drink of water as the icicles hanging from the Krell's garage melted.

Then he flew to the top of the house where he could see almost to the end of the block.

The chickadees and finches had discovered the bread crumbs outside the Krell's back door, the big starlings were fighting over something on the ground up the street, and a faint rat-tat-tat-tat could be heard coming from the direction of the park. Fletcher called out "CHEE! CHEE!" before going in search of food himself.

Meanwhile, Henry and Meg had located the feeder near the schoolyard and found that it did, indeed, offer sunflower seeds. They were so busy cracking open the seeds that they didn't see another cardinal swoop down from a tall tree. It was Nelson—he attacked Henry and sent him flying into the air. As Nelson began to chase Henry away, Meg threw as many sunflower seeds a she could on to the ground. She was hoping they might at least be able to get to the scattered seeds if Henry could get away from Nelson.

Nelson returned to the feeder alone, however, and shoved Meg off as he helped himself to the seeds that were left. Meg's first thought was to find Henry, so she flew to a nearby housetop and called out to Henry, "CHEER, CHEER, what-what-what-what." Her call was soon answered and Henry, with his handsome red feathers just a bit ruffled, was soon perched next to her.

"I don't know, Meg," said Henry. "That Nelson is a fighter. You would think that with the ice and all, he'd be willing to share just a little."

"Oh, Henry," said Meg, "I was worried about you. Let's forget about Nelson and see if we can find something to eat in the park. I can hear Pete drilling into a tree over there."

"I hear it too, Meg," said Henry. "The ice must have melted enough that he can get a good foothold into the tree bark. I guess we could at least check it out."

Most of the wildlife in the neighborhood were able to find food and, almost more importantly, were able to get drinks of water as well. As the sun set, the air grew colder though, which meant everything would be frozen once again by morning. Each day brought its own surprises, and the birds and animals seemed content to just wait and see.

Monday morning at the Krell house meant that Mr. Krell would go to work.

Water remaining on the streets had frozen into patches of ice overnight, so he was anxious to get an early start. However, to the delight of the children, the schools were still closed.

"Drive carefully, dear," said Mrs. Krell as she handed her husband a pair of gloves, "and call to let me know you got to work safely."

"Don't forget to stop at the hardware store to check out bird feeders and pick up more birdseed, Dad," said Jimmy. "Okay?"

"And what about me?" called Sherry from the top of the stairs, "I need more batteries for my game."

Mr. Krell looked thoughtful and replied, "I'll try to remember all that and if you do go outside, be very, very careful—there is still plenty of ice."

Jimmy went to the telephone and called Donald. Like Jimmy, Donald was concerned about the neighborhood birds and wildlife.

"We only have a small amount of birdseed left, and I'm hoping Dad will bring more home. I don't want to just throw it all on the ice, though," said Jimmy. Then he asked Donald, "Are you putting out any bread crumbs or anything?"

"I did that already," said Donald, "but Chance chased off the birds before I could get him back inside."

"They'll be back," said Jimmy. "I'm thinking that birds need water, too—just like we do—but the water needs to be in something sort of flat and close to the ground so they can get to it."

Donald thought about it and said, "How about a garbage can lid? If I can dig a hole in the ice for the lid handle, it just might be a sturdy platform—what do you think?"

"Hmmm," replied Jimmy, "give it a try and then come over here, and we'll see what else we can do."

While the boys were making their plans, Sherry and her mother were sitting at the kitchen table. Jake hopped on a chair and then climbed up to sit on the window sill where he could see what was going on outside.

"Can Bonnie come over to play?" Sherry asked her mother.

"Everything is frozen again," said Mrs. Krell, "and I wouldn't want her to try walking over here just yet."

"I know," said Sherry, "besides, she might see that dead bird."

"What dead bird?" asked her mother.

"Jimmy and I saw a dead yellow bird in the ice when we were walking home yesterday." said Sherry. "Jimmy said that nature's Mom would take care of it, though."

Mrs. Krell smiled and said, "Oh, you mean Mother Nature."

"That's what I said," replied Sherry.

Her mother sighed and asked, "How about we make some cookies?"

"Oh, boy," said Sherry, "That would be great! But . . . maybe we could make some special cookies that the birds would like."

Just then the doorbell rang. Both Sherry and Jimmy ran to open the front door while Jake jumped down and crouched under the kitchen table. Jimmy knew it was Donald and let him in the door. The little dog, Chance, walked over with Donald, seemingly content to sit on the porch to wait for the boy to return.

"Jimmy," called Sherry as the boys climbed up the stairs to Jimmy's room. "Mom and I want to make some cookies for the birds. What kind of cookies do you think they would like?"

The two boys looked at each other, trying not to laugh. Then Jimmy got serious and had an idea. "Go ask Mom if she has any leftover bacon grease or something like it in the refrigerator. Then see if there is any birdseed left in the big can down in the basement, and let me know. Donald and I will get on the Internet and see if we can find some recipes for making suet feeders."

Sherry had never heard of suet and the idea of bacon grease didn't sound too appealing, so she ran to the kitchen and told her mother what the boys had said.

"Why, yes," said Mrs. Krell, "it just so happens that I do have a can of bacon grease in the refrigerator. You can go check on the birdseed downstairs and bring up a cupful while we wait to see what the boys can find."

Jake was on his way to a sunny spot in the living room and was startled to see a dog sitting on the front porch. 'Oh well,' thought Jake, 'as long as he doesn't come inside, I should be able to stretch out for a nap.'

Jimmy and Donald ran down the stairs with papers in their hands.

"Hey, Mom," said Jimmy, "did Sherry tell you what we were doing?"

"Something about bacon grease and birdseed," replied his mother.

"We found some information on the Internet about making suet feeders for birds," said Donald. "Suet is really animal fat, and it said you could get some from the butcher, but Jimmy and I think the bacon grease just might work. The website said birds like suet because it gives them energy and nutrients to help them get through the winter."

"Here's a bowl," offered Mrs. Krell, "and I do have a can of bacon grease."

"And we have some birdseed," added Sherry when she reached the top of the basement steps.

"Hmmm," said Jimmy, as he scooped the grease out of the can into the bowl.

"It says the suet may have to be softened or melted, so maybe we should heat this up in the microwave."

As Mrs. Krell removed the bowl from the microwave, Donald read the next steps as listed in the recipe.

"Now we add the seeds," said Donald, "and anything else the birds might like."

"Like what?" asked Sherry,

"How about some raisins?" said Donald.

"And oatmeal," added Jimmy.

"Maybe even some peanut butter," said Mrs. Krell.

"Oh, boy!" cried Sherry.

As things were added to the bowl, the glob of grease grew in size and stickiness. Everyone washed their hands and stood, looking at their suet.

"Now what?" asked Mrs. Krell.

"Now we need something to put it in," said Donald. "The website suggested a mesh onion bag or some sort of plastic netting."

"Remember those big oranges that someone sent us for Christmas?" asked Jimmy, looking at his mother. "Each one came in its own red plastic bag—that's like a mesh bag, and I think that might work."

While his mother went to look for the plastic mesh, Jimmy pulled some string and scissors out of a kitchen drawer.

Sure enough, for some odd reason, Mrs. Krell had saved the red plastic mesh holders and soon, the children had divided the suet mix into three of the bags. It was a messy job, but the children were laughing as they all tried to wash their hands at the kitchen sink at the same time.

Donald and Jimmy set to work with the string and scissors, tying the bags closed at the top and leaving plenty of string to fasten them to tree branches.

"See if you can find places to hang the feeders, kids, while I make lunch," said Mrs. Krell. "Just remember to be careful on the ice."

Chance was delighted to see the three children in the Krell's backyard and raced over to see if they were ready to play. Although they didn't seem to want to play, they sure had something in their hands that smelled good to him!

"No, Chance," said Donald. "This isn't for you. Be a good dog, and stay out of the way."

Chance stood his ground and watched as the boys did their best to fasten their new feeders. The icy branches made it impossible to climb very high, however. So Donald would tie a rock to the end of a string and Jimmy would throw it over a high branch. After several tries, it worked, and they were able to pull each mesh bag fairly high and fasten the end of the string on a lower branch.

Sherry stood by Chance and clapped each time a suet feeder was put in place. It was bitterly cold outside, so the children and the dog were ready to head back to the house. As the door shut behind the children, Chance trotted home where he, too, would get fed and warm again.

CHAPTER 7 – AN UNUSUAL DAY

The neighborhood, still trapped in a layer of ice, was quiet. It was sunny, but the breeze that blew through the big spruce tree in the Krell's backyard was cold. The children and dog had scared many of the feathered folk to seek shelter in other trees. Henry and Meg were satisfied to move closer to the trunk of the blue spruce tree and wait for the noise and the children to go away.

Fletcher wasn't one to wait, however. He had watched everything from the housetop and found it all rather interesting. He saw the children go into the house and waited until the dog was halfway up the street to glide down to the swing set. He looked all around, shaking his blue crest, and let out a careful "CHEE!"

The cardinal pair moved out to the edge of their ice-covered branch. They could tell something was different, but didn't know what it might be.

"What do you see, Fletcher?" asked Henry. "Was that dog digging around under the bushes again?"

"Nope," answered Fletcher, "but I see something new—let's check it out."

Henry and Fletcher flew to a branch and looked down at the ball of suet that hung just below, swinging slightly in the breeze. Food! Soon, Meg and the usual collection of finches, sparrows, and chickadees were all enjoying the suet, raisins, and seeds. Some clung to the trunk of the small trees to reach the source of food, and some hung upside down from the branch. The smaller chickadees were able to cling to the webbing and dive right in. A goldfinch reported a tray of water available halfway up the block, and many of the birds flew over to get a drink before it, too, was frozen.

Henry and Meg were still digging through the suet to pick out the seeds when they heard Fletcher's warning call. They flew to the top of a small tree, trying to see what was going on and there he was—Mr. Trouble, dressed in a similar cloak of red feathers—Nelson! Ever protective of his territory, Henry flew at the intruder, trying to drive him away. Nelson did fly away, but then circled around and landed on the swing set. Henry stood guard over the suet feeders as if daring his enemy to come near.

"Wait a minute," said Nelson. "I'm not here to cause trouble."

"Good," said Henry, "then go away."

"I'm here for . . . that is . . . I need help, and I'm willing to call a truce."

"What's this about a truce?" squawked Fletcher, perching on the end of the swingset bar. "Do you mean you're not here to fight?"

"No, not really," said Nelson. "I came to ask for help because I didn't know where else to go. So just listen, okay?"

Henry was still ready to defend himself, but said, "Okay, what do you need?"

"It's Singer," said Nelson. "She's ill or something. I think the cold has really hit her hard this year. I can't get her to leave our night spot across from the school, and the feeder there is empty. We've been together for two years now and spring is almost here, but I think if she can get some food and water, she might improve."

"Oh, yes," chirped Meg, "some of this suet and a few seeds might be just the thing for Singer. Maybe we could just carry some of it over to her—just this once."

Henry stood still, but didn't say anything. Fletcher spoke up, "Gee, Henry, I'd be willing to help just this once, like Meg said."

"Well," said Henry, "okay—just this once—but it doesn't mean we're friends or anything, right?"

"Right," agreed Nelson. "If we each take just a bit of suet and seeds to my poor Singer, I'm sure she'll get better."

"Let's go," said Fletcher.

The three birds didn't say another word as they filled their beaks with suet, raisins, and seed. They then followed Nelson as he flew to his mate. Singer was huddled low on a tree branch behind one of the houses across from the school. The cardinal pair and the bluejay alighted on a nearby bush, giving Nelson a chance to speak to Singer.

"Here," encouraged Nelson, "I brought suet for you. You need to eat something."

Singer's eyes peered at her mate as if he had arrived from another planet. "What?" she said weakly. "Where would you find any suet?" Then she took a bit of the suet and swallowed. When she had finished all that Nelson could carry, she gazed at the empty feeder and said, "I guess that's all there is, isn't it?"

"Not really," replied Nelson. "I knew it wouldn't be enough, so I found some other birds that were willing to bring you food as well. I'll call them over and sit right next to you on this branch—you don't have to be afraid."

When the three friends heard Nelson's call, they flew to a closer branch, and one at a time, offered Singer what they had carried in their beaks. At first Singer was timid, especially with the big bluejay, but she was even more amazed to have Henry there. Having eaten her fill, it didn't take long for at least some of her energy to return, and her eyes appeared bright again.

"How can I possibly thank each of you?" said Singer. "I'm sure I can make it through the night now, and maybe it will start to get warm again soon."

"Glad you're better, Singer," said Fletcher, "but don't start spreading the word around about me. Everyone thinks I'm just a noisy jay who interferes in their lives, and that's okay with me. I've got to keep up my tough image, if you know what I mean."

"Sure, Fletcher," said Nelson, "we understand. I won't ask anything else of you, but thanks again."

As Fletcher flew off, Henry and Meg prepared to leave as well. Meg hesitated a moment and said to Singer, "Have Nelson find me if you need anything else. Henry and I have been together two years, too, so I can only imagine how your Nelson must have felt."

"Thanks, Meg," chirped Singer, "let's just hope that spring arrives soon."

"Okay, that's enough," said Nelson, "I know we can't really be friends, but you two really made a difference and . . . well . . . I just want to say thanks."

Meg and Henry said their good-byes and flew back to their spruce tree. They stopped for a drink of water from the trash can lid behind the blue house, but it had frozen over. It was getting dark, so the birds and wildlife of the neighborhood would have to wait and hope the ice would begin to melt soon. The cardinal pair looked longingly at the pole sticking up from the ground in the Krell's backyard where the bird feeder once sat and settled in for the night. It had certainly been an interesting and unusual day.

Chapter 8 – Choosing a Feeder

Sherry was playing with Jake on the stairs, so she was the first to hear the sound of the car entering the garage.

"Daddy's home!" she shouted, which sent Jake racing up the stairs to hide under the closest bed he could find.

Sherry had the door open by the time Mr. Krell, carrying a shopping bag in each hand, walked carefully up the front steps. His wife came into the hallway, drying her hands on a dishtowel, and Jimmy ran down the stairs to join the family.

"Oh boy," said Jimmy as he peered into the heavy bag that his father had put on the floor, "birdseed—and the kind with dried berries, too, which is just what we need."

"And flowers for my lady," said Mr. Krell as he gave them to Mrs. Krell with a smile and slight bow. "I thought they might add a bit of color to these dreary days."

Mrs. Krell was about to respond, but Sherry spoke first.

"What about me, Daddy, did you get the batteries like I asked?"

"Well, now," answered Mr. Krell, "I don't see any batteries, but I seem to remember picking some up while I was at the hardware store. Hmmm—where did I put them?"

"Look in your pockets," said Sherry, and she tried to be helpful.

"That's a good idea, Little One," said Mr. Krell, "although maybe I left them in the car."

"I'll go look," said Sherry, and she started out the front door.

"Hold on there," said Mr. Krell, "I think I feel something rather heavy in this pocket."

Sherry lifted the flap over the pocket on her father's winter coat and reached inside.

"I found them! I found them!" she squealed with delight. Then she remembered her manners and said, "Thanks, Dad, now I can play my game again."

Sherry fled up the stairs, and Mrs. Krell took the flowers to the kitchen. Mr. Krell hung up his coat and told Jimmy that the roads were okay, but everything was still frozen.

"Ah, Dad . . . did you happen to look at bird feeders while you were in the hardware store today?" asked Jimmy.

Father and son walked to the family room where Mr. Krell sat down in his favorite chair and heaved a sigh of relief.

"As a matter of fact, I did," said Mr. Krell. "There is certainly an assortment of styles and prices. I saw several different kinds that would fit nicely on the pole in the backyard, too."

Jimmy's eyes lit up, but his father went on to say, "I wanted to see what you found on the Internet though, before we make a decision."

Jimmy enjoyed the fact that his father was seeking his input and that they were having a very adult conversation.

"Okay, Dad," said Jimmy. "Sit here while I get the list of the feeders I thought would be best. I printed out some pictures, too."

Mr. Krell gladly relaxed and closed his eyes for a moment. He was thinking of the upcoming baseball season when he heard Jimmy bounding down the stairs.

"Here's what I found, Dad," said Jimmy as he quickly threw books and magazines off the coffee table and began to lay out the pages he had printed out earlier that day.

Mr. Krell bent forward to look things over, but didn't say anything.

"You know, Dad," said Jimmy, "we have a variety of birds around here. The little finches, sparrows, juncos, and chickadees eat the smaller seeds, but the bigger birds, like the cardinals and mourning doves, prefer the bigger seeds and berries—especially the sunflower seeds. Even that pesky bluejay seems to spend a lot of time at the feeder."

"So what do you think would work to satisfy that crowd?" asked Mr. Krell.

"A good feeder needs a rim of some kind on at least two sides where the birds can perch while they feed. It's best if the roof sticks out enough to offer a bit of cover when it's raining or snowing. Now if we had one that was big enough, we would only have to fill it up once a day. Oh, and it has to be built well and sturdy enough to take a few hits from ice balls and last a long time."

"You've certainly done your homework, son," said Mr. Krell, "let's look at some of these pictures and sort them out to narrow down our choices."

Jake was interested, too. He hopped up on the coffee table and had just started walking over all the papers when Jimmy picked him up and placed him back on the floor. The disappointed cat decided the only place left for a cat to go was the kitchen.

A short while later, Mrs. Krell called Sherry to put silverware on the table and fill the water glasses for dinner. It was dark and cold outside as the family gathered for dinner, but the colorful flowers brought thoughts of spring. Mr. Krell said grace, and there was plenty of dinner table conversation—mostly about the icy weather, birds, and the suet feeder project. Jake was content laying on the floor with his front paws tucked under his chest. He liked to have his people all in one place.

The family's evening routine consisted of Jimmy rinsing the dishes and stacking them in the dishwasher and Sherry putting food in Jake's bowl before doing her schoolwork. While the children were thus occupied, their parents took steaming cups of tea into the family room to read the newspaper and catch up on their day.

It didn't take long for Jimmy to race through his chores so he and his father could get back to the job of choosing just the right bird feeder. After much discussion and paper shuffling, a decision was reached.

"This is the one," said Jimmy. "It's plenty big, and I like the fact that it's square and has four sides from which the birds can eat."

"How do you open it to add the seed?" asked his father.

"Look," said Jimmy, "the pointed roof is hinged, so all I'd have to do would be to open one side and pour in the seed. Neat, huh?"

"I'll have to admit," said Mr. Krell, "that the design is very good and because it's made of natural cedar, it should hold up well."

"And the sides are made of strong acrylic so I can see when it's empty," said Jimmy with excitement in his voice. "And did you read where there's a screen on the bottom to allow any water to drain and let the air in? It's really the best."

"Well," said Mr. Krell slowly, "I saw one like it in the hardware store, but there is one little problem."

"I know," said Jimmy sadly, "it's too expensive. But it has everything, and you know how much I enjoy watching and learning about the birds that visit our backyard."

"I do know," responded Mr. Krell, "and I'm proud of you, son, and . . . well, we'll just have to think about it."

"We don't have much time, Dad," said Jimmy. "If this ice doesn't melt, the birds won't make it. I don't want to lose any of them."

Jimmy and his father sat quietly for a moment. Then Jimmy offered an idea. "I have some money saved up from my birthday, and I'll put it toward the feeder—would that help?

"I'm sure it would, son," said his father, "but that gives me an idea. I'm thinking there might just be a way of getting that feeder yet."

Chapter 9 – Mr. Krell's Plan

Mr. Krell told Jimmy what he was thinking, and they agreed that his plan was the answer they had been looking for.

"You don't think it is too late to get started now, do you, Dad?" Jimmy asked.

"Not really," said Mr. Krell. "This is pretty important. If you need my help, just ask."

Jimmy jumped up and ran to the telephone. He called both Sam and Ralph and asked them to come to his house right away for a meeting. Sam said he still had homework to do, and Ralph thought it was getting too late to be walking down the street. Jimmy informed them that it was very important and if the boys had trouble getting their parents' permission, Jimmy's father would be glad to talk with them. Sam and Ralph were curious and suspicious at the same time, so they agreed to be at the Krell's house as soon as possible.

While Jimmy was on the telephone, Mr. Krell shared the plan with his wife. Mrs. Krell thought it was a great idea and said she'd make sure Sherry was kept busy while the meeting took place in the living room.

Sam and Ralph had told their parents that they were needed at the Krell's house to help Jimmy with a project, then walked down the street together. They couldn't even guess what it was all about, but thought it might have something to do with the snowball fight.

Mr. Krell and the three boys were soon seated in the living room, munching on cookies that Mrs. Krell had provided.

"Jimmy and I need your help," said Mr. Krell as he addressed Sam and Ralph. "You must know that I was very angry when I heard about the ice balls you two were throwing at my son and his friend."

Sam and Ralph looked at each other and sunk down in their chairs. Sam spoke up first, saying, "We're sorry that Jimmy got hurt, Mr. Krell."

"Yeah," said Ralph, "I guess it wasn't such a good idea, and maybe we didn't know our own strength."

"Strength has nothing to do with it, boys," replied Mr. Krell with a very serious look on his face. "Your actions were thoughtless and dangerous. I think you will agree that there ought to be some sort of punishment."

Sam and Ralph nodded their heads, but couldn't think of anything to say.

"Now I'll agree not to tell your parents about all this if you agree to help Jimmy and me with something."

Sam and Ralph, still silent, eagerly nodded their heads as they wondered what would be required of them.

"Okay," said Mr. Krell, "here's the story. I don't know if you boys are aware of the fact that my son has an avid interest in wildlife and birds in particular. One of your ice balls destroyed the feeder in our backyard. Now, it was getting old, but it may have lasted another winter. Jimmy and I have found a new, strong bird feeder that Jimmy thinks would be the very best for the birds in our neighborhood."

Jimmy got up and gave Ralph the picture of the feeder, and the older boys seemed to study it thoroughly. They gave the picture back to Jimmy and waited.

Mr. Krell continued to explain the plan. "This particular feeder is expensive and since you two broke our original feeder, we feel that you should help pay for a new one."

"Yes, sir," said Sam and Ralph added, "I don't have much money, but I'll give you what I have if that will help."

"That's a start," said Mr. Krell, "but I'm thinking there is a way for you both to earn the additional money needed to pay for a good portion of the feeder. All this ice should start to melt soon. You are both strong enough to start shoveling the icy porches and sidewalks around this block and as far as you're willing to go. I would suggest you talk to the home owners and offer to shovel their walkway and driveway without asking for any money. Now, if they want to pay you something for your work, anything you receive would be given to me to put toward the new feeder."

Mr. Krell stopped talking and waited for a response. Sam and Ralph were quiet, too, thinking it all over. They looked at each other and appeared to be in agreement.

"Okay," said Sam, "we'll do it."

"But you won't tell our parents about the deal, right?" asked Ralph.

"As long as you keep your part of the bargain, I won't tell them," replied Mr. Krell.

"We can do it," said Sam. "We'll just tell our parents that we decided to do something good for the neighbors."

Ralph smiled and said, "Yeah—they'll be shocked!"

The boys had a good laugh over that, and Jimmy couldn't help but laugh, too. Imagine Sam and Ralph, doing something good, how cool was that?!

Mr. Krell wasn't quite finished. "Now I stopped by the hardware store today to look at bird feeders," he said, "and I picked up some brochures on the things that birds need to survive the winter in our area. It describes various types of bird feeders, seed, and how the birds need water in the winter months as well. There's a lot of information in the brochures, and I'm thinking that as you shovel out the neighborhood, you could also distribute the brochures. It would be a way of getting other households involved."

Sam and Ralph each took a handful of brochures and started looking through them. Jimmy smiled proudly at his father and said,

"We can get more of those if you run out, and if you two want to work with Donald and me, maybe the four of us could get some birdhouse kits or even design our own."

It was Mr. Krell's turn to smile at his son. His plan seemed to be working—so far. He would have to keep an eye on Sam and Ralph and make sure they did their part.

Sam and Ralph were barely out the door and on their way home when Jimmy called Donald to report on his father's plan.

"Wow," laughed Donald, "I can't wait to see Sam and Ralph shoveling walkways up and down the street! Now tell me about this feeder that you like. If it's expensive and we have to wait for the money to come in, it will be summer by the time we get the feeder."

"I'll talk with Dad. I bet I can get him to buy the feeder tomorrow, and the money that comes in from Sam and Ralph will go toward paying him back."

"Okay," said Donald, "It looks like the school will be open tomorrow, and I have to study for a math test, so I'll see you later."

Chapter 10 – The Big Thaw

By the time Jimmy and Sherry arrived at the breakfast table the next morning, their father was standing near the sink, gulping down a final cup of coffee. "I'm going to work early," he announced, "so I can leave early and stop by the hardware store to pick up the bird feeder on my way home. Maybe we can get it mounted before it gets dark outside."

"Thanks for going along with my idea about getting the feeder now, Dad," said Jimmy. "I can put some birdseed on the ground this morning, but I know the birds will feel safer when the new feeder is set up."

The children were anxious to go back to school and meet with their friends again, so Mrs. Krell didn't even have to remind them to get their school supplies ready. She stood outside the front door and watched as they made their way past the blue spruce tree and walked carefully around the patches of ice on the sidewalk. The sun was shining and although everything was still frozen, the TV weather man had promised that it would finally be warm enough to melt the remaining ice.

As Mrs. Krell went back into the warm house, Jake slipped by her and found a dry spot on the front porch where he could sit, sniff the air, and see what was happening in the neighborhood.

The birds didn't need a weather man to tell them that the ice would soon be melting. They could feel the slightest change in temperature as the sun rose higher in the sky, and they knew it was the beginning of the end of the ice. Fletcher had reported that the water in the pan behind the blue house was still frozen, so it was just a matter of waiting.

Henry and Meg had joined their feathered friends on the ground of the Krell's backyard. They were delighted to find a nice supply of sunflower seeds had been thrown out with the smaller seeds and even some dried berries. It was still icy, so there was much slipping and sliding as birds big and small went after the seed.

"Watch it!" chirped a chickadee as a goldfinch bumped into him. The goldfinch grabbed a few seeds and flew to the top of a bush and sang just a bit of her song before descending back to the ground.

The noise and movement had caught the attention of Jake. He just had to see what was going on in his own backyard. He crouched down low and crept across the driveway to one of his favorite hiding places under low bush. What he saw was constant movement of colors and feathers. Birds were flying back and forth from the trees to the ground—and there were so many birds!

Fletcher was on the lookout from the top of the garage, but didn't notice the orange cat under the bush. He was watching Pete, who clung to the trunk of one tree, then glided to another tree where he was pecking away at the rough bark.

Henry flew from the blue spruce tree and landed next to Fletcher. "Quite a sight," said Henry, referring to the feeding frenzy.

"Yup," replied Fletcher, "soon all the seed will be gone, but at least everyone will have had something to eat. No water, though. This ice had better start melting soon."

Henry let out his call, "CHEE!, CHEE!, what-what-what-what," as he tried to get Meg's attention. Pete was the one who turned his head, however, and flew to join his friends on top of the garage.

"Hey, hey," said Pete, "I came over to check out the suet bags, but there's not a drop of the good stuff left. Too bad, too bad."

"It went fast," said Fletcher. "when this batch of seed is gone, we'll have to start looking for food elsewhere."

"Maybe the boy will bring out more seed later today," said Henry, hopefully.

"I don't know," said Pete, "I saw all the neighborhood kids walking to school this morning. You don't suppose they'll forget about us, do you—do you?"

"I'm thinking the ice will start to melt today," said Henry, "and that should help more than anything else."

"Me, too—me, too" said Pete, who had a habit of repeating short phrases. Maybe it was all that hammering with his bill.

"Come on, Pete," sang Henry, "let's fly over to the park and see what we can find."

Jake watched the two big birds fly away and decided it was a good thing. It was the smaller birds that were easier to catch. Now, if he could just sneak up on them.

The sun was indeed slowly getting stronger. The little birds didn't seem to notice that the ice was beginning to soften under their feet as they chased after the last bit of birdseed on the ground. Jake knew his time was limited, so he bunched his muscles under his fur and dashed out of his hiding place and across the frozen yard.

"CHEE! CHEE!" called Fletcher. The remaining juncos, finches, and chickadees flew up into the trees as the orange cat raced around in circles. Jake was slipping and sliding on the ice and jumped into the air in a final attempt to grab a mouth full of feathers. When he landed on the ice, it broke up into pieces, causing him to roll over on his side. He gained his footing just in time to race under his favorite bush before the big bluejay could sink that sharp bill into his fur.

Fletcher flew to the top of the swingset and let out several more warning calls as he searched the yard for the cat. Then all was quiet—very quiet. Jake waited for his breathing to return to normal before leaving his spot under the bush. Then he slowly walked across the driveway acting as if nothing had happened and curled up on the front porch, hoping the door would open soon.

By afternoon the melting of the ice had begun in earnest. The dripping from icicles and the sound of water running across the streets and sidewalks was music to the wildlife. Henry and Meg found a small pool of water in a nearby driveway and after getting much needed drinks, they were even able to do a bit of feather cleaning as well.

The afternoon melt meant fun for the children returning home from school as well. Sherry and Bonnie splashed through every puddle of water they could find while the older boys took turns sliding on the leftover ice.

Two of the older boys didn't take time to play, however. Sam and Ralph raced home, grabbed their shovels, and began going from house to house, offering to clear sidewalks and driveways.

Jimmy and Donald strolled up the street, watching the good-deed-boys at work.

"I think you missed a spot," called out Jimmy. "You two have to get done as much as possible before this water freezes again overnight."

"Lay off, Jimmy," said Ralph. "Can't you see we're busy? We'll stick to our part of the bargain, don't you worry."

"Okay, okay," said Jimmy, "We'll let you alone." Then he turned to Donald and said, "Let's go to my house and see if my dad is home yet. He said he'd try to get home with the new bird feeder early so we could put it up before dark."

As the boys entered the back door of the Krell's house, they could see two pairs of very wet pants, socks, and boots sitting on the basement stairs.

"Looks like Sherry and Bonnie went swimming on their way home from school," commented Jimmy, with a smile.

"Let's go to your room before they know we're home," suggested Donald.

A very worn out cat was sprawled out on the kitchen floor, but didn't even bother to move a whisker as the boys stepped over him. Jake was sure there would be warmer, drier, happier days ahead.

Soon Mr. Krell arrived home with a cardboard box under his arm. Jimmy and Donald met him anxiously at the front door.

"Is that it, Dad? Is that the feeder?" asked Jimmy.

"This is it, son, and I'm glad you're here, too, Donald," said Mr. Krell. "This is one of those things we have to put together. My friend Joe, who works at the hardware store, said it should all go well if we just followed the instructions."

Jimmy took the box into the living room and instantly began to spread the pieces of wood and plastic over the coffee table. Mr. Krell sat in his favorite chair and read the directions out loud.

The boys sorted things out and began fitting and snapping the pieces into place. At one point, Jimmy ran to the kitchen to get a screwdriver while his father rechecked the work. In less than an hour, the completed bird feeder was sitting on the table with only the bolts needed to fasten it to the pole left over.

"Oh, my gosh," said Donald, "This is fantastic!" Look at the sturdy rails and the hinged roof."

"And look," said Jimmy, "there's a screen on the bottom for dirt or any water to go through. It sure looks strong to me."

"There's just one thing left to do." added Mr. Krell, "I'm going to get a wrench and it's dark enough that we'll need a flashlight, but we'll have the feeder up and running in no time.

Chapter 11 – A New Day

Once the sun was up and shining brightly the next day, the remaining ice continued to melt. But it wasn't the dripping of the icicles that caught the attention of the feathered folk in the neighborhood. It was a new feeder—the most beautiful sight in the world that caused the excitement.

Fletcher, of course, was the first to notice the difference and instead of the usual warning call, he let out a song. The sound drew Henry and Meg to the edge of a branch in the blue spruce tree, where they, too, stared in wonder.

"So that's what the people were doing in the yard last night," chirped Henry.

"Let's check it out," added Meg, and the cardinal pair were the first to try out the feeder and found how easy it was to pick out the sunflower seeds and dried berries.

It didn't take long for the smaller birds to discover the new feeder as well and with four sides available to perch, there was very little fighting for places, until . . .

"Hey, scram!" called Fletcher as Nelson and Singer landed on the feeder. "CHEE! CHEE! CHEE! CHEE!" went out the warning cry.

Henry and Meg were enjoying a drink of water from the melting ice and flew to a branch before even looking to see what danger was at hand.

"It's that Nelson fellow," said Henry in an angry tone, "I'll show him!"

Meg followed as Henry flew to the feeder and tried to bump Nelson off. Nelson flew to the other side and tried to pick up a sunflower seed, but Henry flew over the top of the feeder and pecked Nelson on his head as he flew by. All the other birds gave the cardinals plenty of room to fight it out, but it was Fletcher who stood on top of the feeder and tried to settle things.

"Look, Henry," said the jay, "there seems to be plenty of room here. Why don't you let Nelson and Singer feed on this side while you and Meg are on the other side?"

"They're not even part of our neighborhood, Fletch," said Henry. "Nelson came here just to pick a fight."

"There seems to be plenty of seeds and berries," said Meg. "Let's let them have their fill, just this one time. I'm sure that with the ice now melting the other feeders over by the school yard will be filled soon."

"Just stay on that side, then" said Henry, "but I'll be watching you."

With the warm sunshine and melting ice, the neighborhood became much quieter. The streets were clear of ice and slush, and the children were able to walk to school on bare sidewalks once again. Jake had been sitting on the front porch of the house until Chance trotted by, then he quietly slipped into his favorite hiding place under the bushes. Squirrels ventured out of their nests and were able to dig through the soft ground in search of previously buried nuts.

The feathered folk were enjoying the warm sunshine, full tummies, and fresh water. It was time to begin thinking about finding mates, building nests, and greeting old friends who would soon be returning from the south. Nuts, seeds, and berries had provided nourishment during the cold, winter season, but Mother Nature was even now preparing a fresh crop of soft seeds, insects, bugs, and worms for birds of all colors and sizes. It was a good time to be a bird.

THE END

Vine Street

Maple Street

Sherwood Street

Douglas

Chalmer
Ben, Nancy

Tillman
(Midnight)

Thurber
Amy, Joey, Carl

Benchley
Daryl

Frost
Donald (Chance)

Nelson
Bonnie

Langley
Susan, Carol

Johnson
Matthew

Newman

Thomas

Krell
Jimmy, Sherry
(Jake)

Jasper Street

www.ingramcontent.com/pod-product-compliance
Lightning Source LLC
Chambersburg PA
CBHW060241190526
45161CB00001B/10